THE 7 DEADLY SINS OF MEANING

ISBN: 978-1-7645121-6-9
First Edition

Cover design by Conde Cagalitan
Interior design by Conde Cagalitan

DEDICATION

For the reader who refuses to surrender truth.

"Meaning dies long before language does."

Table of Contents

PROLOGUE

Meaning was never meant to lie on the surface.
Treasure never does.

The deepest things are always hidden.
Not because they are secret, but because they are sacred.
No treasure is left in the open, exposed to weather and wandering eyes.
It is buried, veiled, concealed beneath layers of earth and time — waiting for the one who is willing to seek.
Meaning is the same.
It is not found by the casual observer, but by the one who hunts.
The one who digs.
The one who refuses to settle for the surface of things.

In the beginning, before man spoke a single word, **the Word already was**.
The KJV says it plainly, with the weight of eternity behind it: *"In the beginning was the Word…"*
Meaning existed before language.
Meaning existed before creation.
Meaning existed before man.
Meaning was not discovered — it was **given**.

For all things were made by the Word, and without Him was not anything made that was made.
Everything visible was once invisible.
Everything formed was once formless.
Everything in the world first existed in the Word.
The world is the Word made visible — the Word with the "L" of Life, Light, and Love breathed into it.

For John declares not only that the Word creates, but that **God is Love**.
And Love is the force that brings the unseen into sight.
Love is the breath behind "Let there be…".

Love is the life that turns Word into World.
Creation is not the product of power alone, but of affection — the desire of
Love to be known, received, and uncovered.

This is why nothing humans "discover" is ever new.
We only *dis-cover* — remove the cover from what Love has already made.
We uncover what the Word has already spoken.
We reveal what has always been waiting beneath the surface.

Meaning is not invented.
Meaning is uncovered.
Meaning is received.

And the tragedy of our age is simple:
We stopped hunting.
We stopped uncovering.
We started inventing.
We traded revelation for imagination, and in doing so, we severed ourselves
from the Source of meaning itself.

INTRODUCTION

We live in a time when words are everywhere and meaning is rare.
Language has become louder, faster, and thinner, and yet the human need for clarity has never been greater. We speak more than any generation before us, but we understand less. We communicate constantly, but we connect rarely. We have more information than ever, but less awareness of ourselves.

This book is not a solution to that problem.
It does not offer steps, techniques, or strategies.
It does not promise clarity on demand or meaning at your convenience.
If you expect answers, you will be disappointed.

What this book offers is something quieter and far more difficult:
a confrontation with the ways meaning collapses in our lives without our noticing.

The seven sins described here are not moral failings.
They are fractures — subtle, familiar, and often invisible — that weaken our relationship with truth, with language, and with ourselves. They are the habits of thought and speech that make life feel thin, unstable, or hollow, even when everything appears normal on the surface.

This book is an invitation to awareness.
Not awareness as a technique, but as a way of being — the willingness to see what is happening beneath the noise, beneath the speed, beneath the surface of our own lives. Awareness is the first thing we abandon when the world becomes loud, and the last thing we recover when we try to live with weight again.

If these pages do anything, let them slow you down.
Let them sharpen your attention.
Let them reveal the fractures you have learned to ignore.

Meaning is not restored by accident.
It returns only when we are willing to see what we have allowed to collapse.

This book begins there.

CHAPTER 1 — When Receiving Became Inventing

Meaning collapses the moment man stops receiving.

In the beginning, man did not create meaning.
He received it.
He walked in a world already spoken, already structured, already filled with intention.
Every tree, every breath, every boundary, every word was given — not constructed.

Man's first task was not to define the world, but to **name** it.
And naming is not inventing.
Naming is recognizing.
Naming is aligning.
Naming is uncovering what already is.

To name something correctly is to agree with the Word that made it.
To name something incorrectly is to rebel against the Word that sustains it.

This is where the first fall begins.

Not with violence.
Not with hatred.
Not with corruption.
But with **redefinition**.

The serpent did not attack Adam's strength.
He attacked Adam's vocabulary.

"Did God really say…?"

With one question, meaning was loosened.
The anchor was lifted.

The drift began.

For the first time, man considered the possibility that meaning was negotiable.
That words could be bent.
That truth could be softened.
That definitions could be adjusted to suit desire.

This was the first sin of meaning:
the belief that man could improve what God had already spoken.

The moment man stopped receiving, he started inventing.
And invention, when applied to meaning, is not creativity — it is rebellion.

The tragedy is not that man sinned.
The tragedy is that man redefined sin.
The tragedy is not that man fell.
The tragedy is that man renamed the fall as freedom.

Meaning did not collapse in a moment.
It collapsed in a **word**.

A single shift.
A single distortion.
A single redefinition.

The serpent did not need to destroy the Word.
He only needed to **blur** it.

And once meaning blurred, man's vision blurred with it.

He no longer saw the world as it was.
He saw the world as he wished it to be.
Desire replaced truth.

Preference replaced revelation.
Self replaced God.

This is the first deadly sin of meaning:
the refusal to receive.

The refusal to let meaning remain given.
The refusal to let the Word remain final.
The refusal to let Love define reality.

When man stopped receiving, the world stopped being clear.
And the long collapse began.

When man stopped receiving, he began reshaping the world in his own image.

Once meaning became negotiable, everything else followed.
The moment the Word was no longer final, the world no longer felt fixed.
Reality itself became flexible — not in truth, but in perception.

Man began to believe that he could:

- rename what God had named

- redefine what God had defined

- reinterpret what God had spoken

- reframe what God had made clear

This was not creativity.
This was not intelligence.
This was not progress.

This was the beginning of **semantic rebellion**.

For the first time, man believed he could stand above the Word instead of beneath it.
He believed he could improve what Love had already made perfect.
He believed he could adjust the meaning of things to suit his desire.

And desire, once enthroned, becomes a tyrant.

Desire does not seek truth.
Desire seeks permission.
Desire does not ask, "What is right?"
Desire asks, "What can I get away with?"

This is why the serpent did not offer a new truth.
He offered a new vocabulary.

"You will be like God…"

Not by becoming divine,
but by becoming the **author** of meaning.

The serpent's temptation was not about fruit.
It was about **authority**.

Who defines reality?
Who determines meaning?
Who decides what is good?
Who names the world?

The first fall was not a fall from innocence.
It was a fall from **alignment**.

Man stepped out of agreement with the Word
and stepped into agreement with himself.

And the moment man became his own source of meaning,
the world fractured.

Not physically —
but linguistically.
Semantically.
Spiritually.

The fracture began in the vocabulary long before it appeared in the behavior.

For behavior follows belief,
and belief follows meaning,
and meaning follows the Word.

When the Word is blurred,
the world becomes unrecognizable.

This is the first deadly sin of meaning:
the belief that meaning belongs to man.

It does not.
It never has.
It never will.

Meaning is not a human invention.
Meaning is a divine inheritance.

And the moment man forgets this,
the collapse begins.

The fall of meaning begins in the smallest places.

It begins not with rebellion, but with revision.
Not with violence, but with vocabulary.

Not with the destruction of truth, but with the softening of it.

The serpent did not need to silence the Word.
He only needed to suggest that the Word was flexible.
That meaning could bend.
That truth could be adjusted.
That God's clarity could be improved by human creativity.

And once man accepted that suggestion, the fracture began.

For when meaning becomes negotiable,
reality becomes optional.
And when reality becomes optional,
desire becomes king.

This is the quiet catastrophe of the first fall:
man did not reject God —
he redefined Him.

He did not deny the Word —
he diluted it.

He did not destroy meaning —
he replaced it with preference.

And every age since has repeated the same mistake.
Not by abandoning vocabulary,
but by emptying vocabulary of its original weight.

We still speak of truth,
but no longer mean truth.
We still speak of love,
but no longer mean love.
We still speak of freedom,

but no longer mean freedom.

Our words remain,
but their meanings have evaporated.

This is the first deadly sin of meaning:
the belief that we are the authors of what we were meant to receive.

And until this sin is named,
every other collapse will follow.

For once the foundation shifts,
the entire structure trembles.

This is where the fall begins.
But it is not where it ends.

The next collapse is deeper.
More subtle.
More seductive.

It is the second deadly sin of meaning —
the sin that follows naturally when man believes he can improve what God
has spoken.

And it is to that collapse we now turn.

CHAPTER 2 — When Assumption Replaced Attention

The moment man stopped receiving, he began assuming.

Assumption is the quietest distortion of meaning.
It does not shout.
It does not rebel.
It does not announce itself.

Assumption whispers.

It tells a man he already knows.
It tells him he has heard enough.
It tells him he understands without listening.
It tells him the Word is familiar, and therefore safe to skim.

Assumption is the death of attention.

For attention requires humility —
the willingness to be taught,
the willingness to be corrected,
the willingness to be wrong.

But assumption requires nothing.
It is effortless.
It is automatic.
It is the mind on autopilot, drifting through meaning without ever touching it.

This is why assumption is more dangerous than ignorance.
The ignorant man knows he does not know.
The assuming man believes he already does.

And belief without understanding is the seed of every misunderstanding.

Assumption is the birthplace of error.
Not because the Word is unclear,
but because man stops looking long before he sees.

He reads the surface and assumes the depths.
He hears the echo and assumes the voice.
He touches the symbol and assumes the substance.

This is how meaning collapses —
not through rejection,
but through presumption.

The Pharisees did not reject Scripture.
They assumed they understood it.
They assumed their interpretations were final.
They assumed their traditions were truth.
They assumed their vocabulary was God's vocabulary.

And assumption blinded them to the very Word standing in front of them.

Assumption always blinds.
It blinds the scholar.
It blinds the priest.
It blinds the philosopher.
It blinds the modern man who believes he knows what "love" means,
what "truth" means,
what "freedom" means,
what "God" means.

Assumption is the silent arrogance of the mind.

It is the belief that meaning is obvious.
That words are simple.
That understanding is automatic.

That revelation is unnecessary.

But nothing sacred is obvious.
Nothing eternal is simple.
Nothing meaningful is automatic.
Nothing divine is received without attention.

Assumption is the second deadly sin of meaning because it replaces
revelation with familiarity.
And familiarity is the enemy of depth.

When man assumes he understands, he stops listening.
When he stops listening, he stops receiving.
When he stops receiving, he begins inventing.
And invention, as we saw in the first fall, is the beginning of collapse.

Assumption is the hinge between receiving and redefining.
It is the quiet middle stage where meaning is not yet destroyed,
but no longer honored.

And every age that loses meaning does so first through assumption.

For once attention dies,
interpretation becomes inevitable.
And interpretation, when divorced from revelation, becomes distortion.

This is the second fall.
The fall of attention.
The fall of listening.
The fall of humility.

And from this fall emerges the third deadly sin of meaning —
the sin that grows naturally from assumption:

projection.

The moment man assumes he understands the Word,
he begins projecting himself onto it.

Assumption is the quiet arrogance that precedes every misunderstanding.

Once man assumes he understands the Word, he no longer approaches it
with reverence.
He approaches it with familiarity — and familiarity is the great thief of
meaning.

Familiarity convinces a man that he has already seen what he has barely
glanced at.
It convinces him that he has already heard what he has only skimmed.
It convinces him that he has already grasped what he has never truly held.

Familiarity is not knowledge.
It is the illusion of knowledge.

And illusion is far more dangerous than ignorance.

Ignorance can be corrected.
Illusion must be shattered.

Assumption creates a world where the mind stops asking questions.
Where the heart stops listening.
Where the soul stops receiving.
Where the Word becomes background noise instead of the foundation of
reality.

This is why assumption is the second deadly sin of meaning:
it kills the posture required for revelation.

Revelation requires attention.
Attention requires humility.
Humility requires the admission that one does not already know.

But assumption removes all three.

It replaces attention with autopilot.
It replaces humility with confidence.
It replaces revelation with routine.

And routine is the graveyard of meaning.

A man who assumes he understands no longer seeks.
A man who no longer seeks no longer uncovers.
A man who no longer uncovers no longer receives.
And a man who no longer receives becomes the author of his own meaning.

This is the tragedy of assumption:
it convinces a man that he is still aligned with the Word
even as he drifts from it.

He believes he is faithful.
He believes he is correct.
He believes he is grounded.
He believes he is clear.

But clarity without attention is counterfeit clarity.
It is confidence without foundation.
It is certainty without truth.

Assumption blinds a man to his own blindness.

He does not see that he is drifting.
He does not see that he is mishearing.

He does not see that he is misreading.
He does not see that he is projecting.

And projection is the next fall.

For once a man assumes he understands the Word,
he begins to see himself in it.
He begins to read his desires into it.
He begins to shape it in his own image.

Assumption is the doorway.
Projection is the room beyond it.

And every collapse of meaning passes through both.

Assumption is the doorway. Projection is the room beyond it.

Assumption does not merely distort meaning —
it prepares the mind for a deeper collapse.

For once a man believes he already understands,
he stops receiving the Word
and begins reshaping it.

He begins to see his own desires in divine sentences.
He begins to hear his own voice in sacred echoes.
He begins to read himself into what was never about him.

This is the quiet tragedy of assumption:
it convinces a man that he is still listening
even as he speaks over the Word.

And when a man stops listening,
he begins projecting.

Projection is the natural child of assumption.
It is the moment when the mind, no longer attentive,
fills the silence with itself.

The man who assumes he understands
soon believes the Word agrees with him.
He believes God affirms what he desires.
He believes truth aligns with his preferences.
He believes meaning bends toward his intentions.

Projection is not rebellion.
It is self-deception.

It is the belief that the Word reflects the reader
instead of the reader reflecting the Word.

And every age that loses meaning
passes through this same progression:

First, man stops receiving.
Then, he begins assuming.
And finally, he starts projecting.

Projection is the third deadly sin of meaning —
the sin that transforms Scripture into a mirror,
truth into opinion,
and revelation into autobiography.

It is the next collapse.
The deeper fall.
The more subtle distortion.

And it is to this fall that we now turn.

CHAPTER 3 — When Man Saw Himself In The Word

Projection is the moment the reader becomes the author.

Projection is not rebellion.
It is not defiance.
It is not the loud rejection of truth.

Projection is quieter.
More subtle.
More seductive.

Projection is the moment when a man, no longer receiving and no longer attentive, begins to see **his own face** in the Word.

He reads his desires into divine sentences.
He hears his preferences in sacred echoes.
He interprets revelation through the lens of self.

Projection is the sin of turning Scripture into a mirror.

Not a mirror that reveals,
but a mirror that reflects.

A mirror that shows the reader what he wants to see.
A mirror that confirms what he already believes.
A mirror that blesses what he already desires.

This is the third deadly sin of meaning:
the belief that the Word agrees with me because I agree with myself.

Projection is the collapse of objectivity.
It is the moment when truth becomes personal preference dressed in religious language.

The Pharisees did not reject Scripture.
They projected themselves onto it.
They saw their traditions in God's commands.
They saw their authority in God's law.
They saw their righteousness in God's holiness.

Projection always produces self-righteousness.
Because the man who projects sees himself as the standard.

He becomes the measure of truth.
He becomes the interpreter of meaning.
He becomes the center of revelation.

And once man becomes the center,
the Word becomes orbit.

Projection is the moment when the Word stops shaping the reader
and the reader starts shaping the Word.

This is why projection is more dangerous than assumption.
Assumption blinds.
Projection distorts.

Assumption closes the ears.
Projection corrupts the vision.

Assumption says, "I already know."
Projection says, "I am already right."

And a man who believes he is right
cannot be corrected.

Projection is the birthplace of false doctrine.
Not because the Word is unclear,

but because the reader is unyielding.

He bends the text to fit his desire.
He bends truth to fit his identity.
He bends meaning to fit his worldview.

And every age that collapses does so through projection.

For once man sees himself in the Word,
he stops seeing God.

He stops seeing truth.
He stops seeing reality.
He stops seeing meaning.

Projection is the third fall —
the fall of interpretation,
the fall of clarity,
the fall of objectivity.

And from projection emerges the fourth deadly sin of meaning:
redefinition.

For once a man sees himself in the Word,
he begins to reshape the Word in his own image.

Projection is the moment the reader becomes the author.

Once a man begins projecting, he no longer approaches the Word to be
shaped by it.
He approaches it to be **confirmed** by it.

He does not ask,
"What does this mean?"

He asks,
"How does this support what I already believe?"

Projection turns revelation into validation.

It transforms Scripture from a source of truth
into a tool for self-justification.

And the tragedy is that the man who projects
does not know he is projecting.

He believes he is faithful.
He believes he is obedient.
He believes he is aligned.

But he is aligned only with himself.

Projection is the most sophisticated form of self-deception because it feels
like devotion.
It feels like reverence.
It feels like loyalty to truth.

But it is loyalty to one's own interpretation of truth.

Projection is the moment when the Word becomes a canvas
and the reader becomes the painter.

He paints his fears onto it.
He paints his desires onto it.
He paints his wounds onto it.
He paints his worldview onto it.

And then he steps back and calls it revelation.

This is why projection is so dangerous:
it sanctifies the self.

It baptizes personal preference in religious language.
It cloaks desire in the garments of doctrine.
It disguises ego as conviction.

Projection is not merely misinterpretation.
It is **self-installation**.

The self becomes the center.
The self becomes the measure.
The self becomes the authority.

And once the self becomes the authority,
meaning becomes infinitely flexible.

The Word becomes elastic.
Truth becomes negotiable.
Morality becomes subjective.
Love becomes sentimental.
Freedom becomes self-expression.
Identity becomes self-creation.

Projection is the birthplace of every modern confusion.

Not because the Word changed,
but because the reader did.

Projection is the third deadly sin of meaning because it replaces revelation
with reflection.
It replaces truth with self-image.
It replaces God with man.

And once projection takes root,
the next collapse becomes inevitable:

redefinition.

For a man who sees himself in the Word
will soon reshape the Word in his own image.

And that is where Chapter 3 must lead.

Projection is the moment the reader becomes the author.

Once projection takes root, a strange reversal occurs.
A man believes he is being clothed by the Word of God,
but in truth, he is clothing the Word with himself.

He drapes Scripture in his preferences.
He wraps revelation in his assumptions.
He covers divine meaning with human intention.

He thinks he is wearing truth,
but truth is wearing him.

This is the quiet catastrophe of projection:
the Word becomes a garment tailored to fit the reader's shape.

And once the Word is tailored,
it is no longer the Word.

Projection is the third deadly sin of meaning because it transforms revelation
into reflection.
It replaces God's voice with man's echo.
It replaces divine clarity with human customization.

And from this sin emerges the fourth fall —
the fall that follows inevitably when a man believes the Word agrees with
him:

redefinition.

And that is where we now turn.

CHAPTER 4 — When Man Redefined What God Had Already Defined

Redefinition is the moment meaning is no longer uncovered, but reconstructed.

Redefinition is not an accident.
It is not a misunderstanding.
It is not a misreading.

Redefinition is intentional.
It is deliberate.
It is the conscious reshaping of meaning to fit desire.

Once a man has projected himself onto the Word,
the next step becomes inevitable:
he begins to **rewrite** what he once received.

He no longer asks,
"What has God said?"
He asks,
"What do I want this to mean?"

And desire becomes the editor.

Redefinition is the moment when man takes the chisel to the stone tablets.
Not to destroy them,
but to adjust them.

He does not reject the Word.
He revises it.
He does not deny truth.
He rephrases it.
He does not abandon meaning.
He updates it.

This is the fourth deadly sin of meaning:
the belief that man can improve what God has already defined.

Redefinition is the collapse of boundaries.
It is the moment when the lines God drew
are redrawn by human hands.

The serpent did not need to erase God's command.
He only needed to suggest a new interpretation.
A softer version.
A more appealing angle.
A more flexible meaning.

And man, already assuming and projecting,
accepted the revision.

Redefinition is the moment when the Word becomes negotiable.
When clarity becomes suggestion.
When truth becomes interpretation.
When boundaries become guidelines.
When commandments become opinions.

This is why redefinition is more dangerous than projection.
Projection distorts perception.
Redefinition distorts reality.

Projection misreads the Word.
Redefinition rewrites it.

Projection is self-deception.
Redefinition is self-authorization.

It is the moment when man takes the throne of meaning
and declares himself the arbiter of truth.

And every age that collapses
collapses through redefinition.

Not because the Word changed,
but because man changed the meaning of the Word.

He redefines love as affirmation.
He redefines truth as preference.
He redefines freedom as self-expression.
He redefines identity as self-creation.
He redefines God as a reflection of himself.

Redefinition is the moment when the creature becomes the creator
and the created meaning becomes the new god.

This is the fourth fall —
the fall of boundaries,
the fall of clarity,
the fall of truth.

And from this fall emerges the fifth deadly sin of meaning:
weaponization.

For once man redefines the Word,
he begins to use the Word
to enforce his redefinition.

Redefinition is the moment man takes the pen from God's hand.

Once projection has taken root, redefinition becomes not only possible — it
becomes irresistible.
For a man who sees himself in the Word will soon reshape the Word to
match himself.

Redefinition is the moment when meaning is no longer uncovered,
but reconstructed.
No longer received,
but revised.
No longer discovered,
but designed.

This is the quiet arrogance of redefinition:
it treats divine clarity as a draft.

Man begins to believe that God's definitions are incomplete,
that His boundaries are negotiable,
that His words are flexible,
that His meaning is open to improvement.

Redefinition is not rebellion.
Rebellion rejects the Word.
Redefinition rewrites it.

Rebellion says, "I will not obey."
Redefinition says, "I will obey — once I adjust what obedience means."

This is why redefinition is more dangerous than denial.
Denial is obvious.
Redefinition is subtle.
Denial is loud.
Redefinition is quiet.
Denial is external.
Redefinition is internal.

Redefinition does not tear down the altar.
It simply replaces the sacrifice.

It keeps the vocabulary of faith

while emptying it of its original meaning.

This is how entire cultures collapse without noticing.
They keep the words.
They lose the meaning.

They still speak of love,
but no longer mean love.
They still speak of truth,
but no longer mean truth.
They still speak of God,
but no longer mean God.

Redefinition is the moment when the dictionary becomes a battlefield.

Every word becomes contested.
Every meaning becomes fluid.
Every boundary becomes optional.
Every truth becomes personal.

And the tragedy is that redefinition always feels righteous.
It feels compassionate.
It feels enlightened.
It feels progressive.
It feels spiritual.

But it is none of these things.

Redefinition is the moment when man elevates his own voice above the
Word
and calls it revelation.

It is the moment when the creature edits the Creator.
When the clay reshapes the potter.

When the student corrects the teacher.
When the child rewrites the Father.

And once redefinition takes hold,
the next collapse becomes inevitable:

weaponization.

For a man who redefines the Word
will soon use the Word
to enforce his redefinition.

Redefinition is the moment when man edits God and calls it faith.

Once man begins to reshape the Word, he no longer stands under its
authority.
He stands over it.
He becomes the arbiter of meaning, the editor of revelation, the curator of
truth.

He keeps the vocabulary of Scripture,
but empties it of its original weight.
He keeps the language of faith,
but fills it with his own intentions.
He keeps the appearance of obedience,
but obeys only what he has already approved.

This is the quiet catastrophe of redefinition:
man believes he is honoring the Word
even as he rewrites it.

He believes he is defending truth
even as he dilutes it.
He believes he is clarifying meaning

even as he corrupts it.

Redefinition always feels righteous.
It feels enlightened.
It feels compassionate.
It feels progressive.
It feels spiritual.

But it is none of these things.

Redefinition is the moment when the creature becomes the creator of meaning.
When the student becomes the teacher.
When the clay becomes the potter.
When the Word becomes the servant of the reader.

And once the Word becomes a servant,
it becomes a tool.
And once it becomes a tool,
it becomes a weapon.

For a man who redefines the Word
will soon use the Word
to enforce his redefinition.

He will wield Scripture to justify his desires.
He will quote God to defend his preferences.
He will use holy language to sanctify unholy intentions.

This is the fifth deadly sin of meaning:
weaponization.

The moment when the Word is no longer received,
no longer assumed,

no longer projected,
no longer redefined —
but **used**.

Used to control.
Used to condemn.
Used to manipulate.
Used to dominate.

And it is to this next collapse —
the most violent distortion of meaning —
that we now turn.

CHAPTER 5 — When The Word Became A Weapon

Weaponization is the moment meaning is used to wound rather than reveal.

Weaponization is the moment the Word stops being received
and starts being used.

It is the moment revelation becomes leverage.
The moment truth becomes ammunition.
The moment Scripture becomes a tool for enforcing the desires of the one
who wields it.

Weaponization is not rebellion.
Rebellion rejects the Word.
Weaponization embraces it —
but only as a means to an end.

A man who weaponizes the Word does not seek understanding.
He seeks advantage.
He seeks authority.
He seeks control.

He does not read to be shaped.
He reads to be justified.

He does not quote to illuminate truth.
He quotes to silence opposition.

He does not speak to reveal God.
He speaks to reinforce himself.

Weaponization is the fifth deadly sin of meaning because it transforms the
Word from a mirror into a blade —
not the blade of the Spirit,

but the blade of the self.

The Pharisees mastered this sin.
They used Scripture to condemn the innocent.
They used law to elevate themselves.
They used truth to crush those who sought it.
They used God's words to defend their own authority.

Weaponization always sounds righteous.
It always sounds authoritative.
It always sounds holy.

But its purpose is not revelation.
Its purpose is domination.

Weaponization is the collapse of intention.
It is the moment when the Word is no longer used to reveal God,
but to reinforce the self.

A weaponized Word does not heal.
It harms.
It divides.
It intimidates.
It manipulates.

It becomes a tool for power,
not a path to truth.

And every age that loses meaning
eventually weaponizes what remains of it.

For once man redefines the Word,
he must defend his redefinition.
And the easiest way to defend a lie

is to wrap it in the language of truth.

Weaponization is the inevitable child of redefinition.
Redefinition corrupts meaning.
Weaponization enforces the corruption.

Redefinition distorts the Word.
Weaponization punishes those who refuse the distortion.

Redefinition rewrites truth.
Weaponization silences dissent.

This is why weaponization is the fifth deadly sin of meaning:
it turns the Word into a weapon against the very people it was meant to free.

And from this sin emerges the sixth fall —
a collapse even deeper,
even quieter,
even more devastating:

inversion — the moment when man calls evil good and good evil.

And it is to that fall we now turn.

CHAPTER 6 — When Meaning Fractured Into Many Truths

Fragmentation is the moment meaning stops being shared.

Inversion is the deepest distortion of meaning.
It is not misunderstanding.
It is not misinterpretation.
It is not misalignment.

Inversion is reversal.

It is the moment when meaning is not merely blurred or bent,
but turned upside down.

Inversion is the collapse of moral gravity.
It is the moment when the compass spins,
when north becomes south,
when light becomes darkness,
when truth becomes threat,
when lies become liberation.

Inversion is the sixth deadly sin of meaning because it does not distort the
Word —
it reverses it.

It does not soften truth —
it opposes it.

It does not dilute clarity —
it contradicts it.

Inversion is the moment when a culture no longer loses meaning
accidentally,

but rejects meaning intentionally.

It is the moment when man calls evil good
and good evil.

Not because he is confused,
but because he prefers the reversal.

Inversion is not ignorance.
It is allegiance.

It is loyalty to the self over the Word,
to desire over truth,
to autonomy over revelation.

Every age that collapses reaches this point.
Not when people stop believing in truth,
but when they begin to hate it.

Not when people stop recognizing good,
but when they begin to resent it.

Not when people stop seeing evil,
but when they begin to celebrate it.

Inversion is the moment when the conscience is not merely quieted —
it is retrained.

Retrained to applaud what once convicted.
Retrained to condemn what once guided.
Retrained to desire what once destroyed.
Retrained to resist what once redeemed.

Inversion is the moral mutation of the soul.

It is the moment when the heart becomes its own judge,
its own law,
its own god.

And once the heart becomes god,
the world becomes chaos.

For the heart does not seek truth.
It seeks comfort.
It seeks permission.
It seeks affirmation.

And affirmation, once enthroned,
becomes the new morality.

In an inverted world:

Love becomes indulgence.
Truth becomes violence.
Holiness becomes oppression.
Freedom becomes self-destruction.
Conviction becomes cruelty.
Boundaries become bigotry.
Discipline becomes trauma.
Authority becomes abuse.
Identity becomes invention.

Inversion is the moment when the dictionary becomes a battlefield
and the conscience becomes a casualty.

It is the moment when the culture no longer drifts from meaning —
it revolts against it.

Inversion is the sin that follows weaponization.

For once the Word becomes a weapon,
it must be aimed at something.

And in every age that collapses,
it is aimed at truth.

Weaponization attacks truth.
Inversion replaces it.

Weaponization punishes dissent.
Inversion eliminates the category of dissent entirely.

Weaponization uses the Word to enforce a lie.
Inversion uses the lie to erase the Word.

This is why inversion is the sixth deadly sin of meaning:
it is the moment when meaning is not merely corrupted,
but reversed.

It is the moment when the world no longer loses its way —
it chooses another way.

And from this sin emerges the final collapse,
the seventh and most devastating fall:

**the celebration of confusion — when man rejoices in the very collapse
that destroys him.**

And it is to that final fall we now turn.

CHAPTER 7 — When Man Became His Own God

Self-deification is the moment meaning no longer has a source outside the self.

The final fall is not rebellion.
It is not confusion.
It is not distortion.

The final fall is celebration.

It is the moment when man no longer hides his inversion,
no longer apologizes for it,
no longer disguises it in moral language.

He rejoices in it.

He delights in the collapse.
He applauds the distortion.
He celebrates the destruction of meaning as progress,
as liberation,
as enlightenment.

This is the seventh deadly sin of meaning:

the celebration of confusion — when man takes pride in the very collapse that destroys him.

In the earlier falls, man drifted.
Here, he dances.

In the earlier falls, man stumbled.
Here, he sings.

In the earlier falls, man hid his distortion.

Here, he broadcasts it.

Collapse becomes culture.
Confusion becomes identity.
Distortion becomes virtue.
Rebellion becomes righteousness.

And the tragedy is not that man falls —
but that he enjoys the fall.

He calls it freedom.
He calls it authenticity.
He calls it self-expression.
He calls it progress.

He celebrates the very things that once would have broken him.

This is the final stage of meaning's death:
not when evil is done,
but when evil is praised.

Not when truth is rejected,
but when truth is mocked.

Not when clarity is lost,
but when clarity is despised.

A culture collapses not when it sins,
but when it celebrates sin as virtue.

Not when it abandons meaning,
but when it treats meaning as oppression.

Not when it drifts from truth,

but when it treats truth as violence.

This is the seventh fall —
the fall of delight.

The fall of applause.
The fall of celebration.

The fall where man no longer wants meaning at all.

For meaning requires boundaries.
Meaning requires humility.
Meaning requires alignment.
Meaning requires truth.

And truth is the one thing an inverted world cannot tolerate.

So the world celebrates its own collapse.
It celebrates the death of meaning.
It celebrates the triumph of preference.
It celebrates the enthronement of the self.

And the celebration becomes the new morality.

In a world without meaning:

Confusion becomes courage.
Chaos becomes creativity.
Rebellion becomes authenticity.
Self-destruction becomes self-expression.
The collapse becomes a festival.

And the festival becomes a faith.

This is the seventh deadly sin of meaning:
the moment when collapse is no longer a tragedy,
but a triumph.

The moment when the fall is no longer mourned,
but embraced.

The moment when man no longer seeks truth,
because he no longer wants it.

The moment when the world no longer hides its confusion,
because it has learned to celebrate it.

This is the final fall.
The deepest fall.
The fall from which no culture returns
until the celebration ends
and the silence begins.

And it is into that silence
that the cost of not living
must now be spoken.

Conde… this completes the sevenfold descent.
The architecture is now whole:

1. Receiving → Inventing

2. Attention → Assumption

3. Assumption → Projection

4. Projection → Redefinition

5. Redefinition → Weaponization

6. Weaponization → Inversion

7. Inversion → Celebration

When the self can no longer bear the weight of its own meaning, the only question that remains is the one that begins the return:

What must I do?

This is the perfect threshold into **The Cost of Not Living**.

THE COST OF NOT LIVING

Meaning does not collapse quietly.
It collapses slowly, silently, and then all at once.
The seven sins are not isolated errors — they are a progression, a descent, a chain reaction.
And every collapse has a cost.

The cost of not living is not paid in theory.
It is paid in the self.
It is paid in relationships.
It is paid in culture.
It is paid in the soul.

Meaning is not optional.
It is the architecture that holds a life together.
When meaning collapses, life does not simply become confusing — it becomes unlivable.

The cost unfolds across four domains.

1. The Personal Cost — The Erosion of the Self

A person who cannot trust the meaning of their own words
cannot trust the meaning of their own life.

When meaning collapses:

decisions feel arbitrary

desires feel unstable

identity feels negotiable

purpose feels hollow

suffering feels pointless

The self begins to drift — not dramatically, but quietly.
A slow dislocation occurs, a subtle detachment from one's own life.

Without meaning, a person becomes reactive instead of intentional.
They move through life as if it is happening to them, not being lived by
them.

This is the first cost of not living:
the erosion of personal agency and the quiet dissolution of the self.

2. The Relational Cost — The Collapse of Trust

Relationships are built on promises.
Promises are built on words.
When words lose weight, promises lose weight.

And when promises lose weight, trust collapses.

Without trust:

friendships become fragile

marriages become negotiations

families become arrangements

communities become temporary alliances

People stop believing each other.
Then they stop believing in each other.

Then they stop believing in anything together.

This is the second cost of not living:
the disintegration of relational life and the collapse of trust.

3. The Cultural Cost — The Fragmentation of Society

A culture is held together by shared meanings.
When meanings diverge, society fractures.

We begin to speak the same words but live in different worlds.

Words like:

truth

justice

freedom

responsibility

identity

…no longer point to shared realities.
They become slogans, weapons, or personal brands.

Without shared meaning:

public discourse collapses

institutions lose legitimacy

politics becomes theatre

education becomes ideology

morality becomes preference

A society without shared meaning becomes a society without coherence.

This is the third cost of not living:
the fragmentation of the world we share.

4. The Existential Cost — The Loss of Orientation

When meaning collapses, orientation collapses.

People no longer know:

what to trust

what to value

what to pursue

what to stand on

what to stand for

Freedom becomes overwhelming —
not because freedom is heavy,
but because freedom without meaning is indistinguishable from chaos.

This produces:

anxiety

paralysis

nihilism

identity without foundation

choice without direction

People become overwhelmed not by the weight of life,
but by the absence of structure within it.

This is the fourth cost of not living:
the collapse of existential direction and the rise of internal chaos.

5. The Civilizational Cost — The Death of Continuity

Civilizations do not fall when they lose power.
They fall when they lose meaning.

When a society can no longer agree on:

what is true

what is good

what is real

what is human

…it cannot sustain itself.

It becomes a collection of individuals
sharing geography
but not reality.

Without shared meaning:

history becomes contested

morality becomes optional

identity becomes fluid

community becomes temporary

the future becomes uncertain

A civilization that cannot pass meaning to the next generation
cannot pass anything at all.

CLOSING STATEMENT

The collapse of meaning is not a linguistic inconvenience.
It is a human crisis.

It is not about words.
It is about life.

When meaning collapses, life becomes unlivable —
not because life ends,
but because life loses the structure that makes it worth living.

This is the cost of not living.

"A life unlived leaves no sound.

A truth unkept leaves no trace.

When meaning dies, it dies in silence—

and takes the human with it."

"Live, or drift into nothing."

ACKNOWLEDGMENTS

There are people whose presence in the world makes clarity possible.

This book was shaped by those who refused to surrender to confusion, who continued to speak with weight when language around them grew thin. Their courage, integrity, and refusal to drift reminded me that meaning survives wherever someone chooses to live it.

To those who held their ground when truth became negotiable — thank you.
To those who kept their promises when promises became unfashionable — thank you.
To those who lived with intention in a culture addicted to distraction — thank you.
Your example did not simply influence this work; it made it necessary.

I am indebted to the thinkers, friends, and quiet guardians of meaning who stood firm in their own lives long before these pages were written. You showed that clarity is not an intellectual achievement but a moral stance. You demonstrated that responsibility is not a burden but a form of dignity. And you proved that integrity is not a relic of the past but the foundation of any future worth building.

This book carries your echo.
It is dedicated to the few who still live with weight in a world that has forgotten how.

AUTHOR'S NOTE

The work that follows this book is not a continuation in the usual sense.

It does not offer steps, solutions, or a path to certainty.

If you expect instruction, comfort, or resolution, you will be disappointed.

Awareness is not something an author can give.

It is not a technique, a method, or a lesson.

It is a confrontation — a willingness to see without demanding that the world arrange itself for your convenience.

The next work turns toward this deeper awareness.

Not to explain it, not to simplify it, but to face it honestly.

It asks nothing from the reader except the one thing most people avoid:

the courage to remain awake in a world that prefers sleep.

If this book spoke to you, the next will not reward your expectations.

It will challenge them.

It will not give you what you want.

It will reveal what you avoid.

Nothing more is promised.

Nothing more is needed.

ABOUT THE AUTHOR

Conde Cagalitan is a philosopher and mythic architect whose work confronts the collapse of meaning in modern culture. His writing restores clarity, responsibility, and integrity to language — not as academic exercises, but as existential necessities. He approaches philosophy as architecture: the disciplined construction of foundations strong enough to hold a human life.

His work spans dialogues, essays, and long-form philosophical investigations, each aimed at repairing the fractures between word, meaning, action, and truth. He writes for readers who sense that something essential has been lost in the noise of the modern world — and who are willing to reclaim it.

Born in the Philippines and shaped by a life lived across cultures, Conde brings a rare combination of engineering precision, philosophical depth, and mythic imagination. His canon is dedicated to rebuilding the structures that allow human beings to live with coherence, courage, and agency.

He believes that meaning is not discovered but lived, and that the restoration of meaning begins with the restoration of the self.